11/05

D0775238

The Sacred Places of Wales: A Modern Pilgrimage

by

Peter Williams

1stBooks – rev. 3/16/01

Preface:

By 410 AD, with the fall of the city of Rome and the collapse of its mighty empire, the lights of Christianity began to be extinguished one by one as the Barbarian hordes swept westwards. Only one beacon of light and hope for the Church remained. In the western peninsula of the British Isles, in what is now called Wales, not only did the Church survive, but it began a movement that eventually revitalized Europe. As the cradle of Celtic Christianity, it was Wales that sent missionaries to Cornwall, Britanny, and Ireland and from there St. Columba brought the faith back to northern Britain and to the Continent. It was in Wales, too, that we can speak of Europe's first university, for at Llanilltud Fawr a great monastic school attracted scholars from many countries, including later saints Illtud, Patrick, Dyfrig, and David. Many of the places connected with the cradle of western Christianity still exist today; among the six cathedrals of Wales are some of the oldest in Britain.

Not all the sacred places of Wales are connected to Christianity, for the land was home to the Druids, the guardians of religion, learning and tradition; before them, great stone monuments attest to the faith of the builders and their desire to communicate with their gods. Some people find sacredness in the monuments to those who led Wales in its fight for independence; others in those who fought for a decent wage and standard of living in the early days of the industrial revolution. The Sacred Places of Wales takes you on a modern pilgrimage to all these places.

Contents:

Introduction:

Many sacred sites in Wales date back to pre-historic times, for they are the neolithic burial chambers. Others are among the earliest Christian sites in Britain.

In the first century A.D. much of Celtic Britain was conquered by Rome, and by the second century, missionaries from Gaul had introduced Christianity into the island, and many of the pagan temples of the Celtic peoples were converted into churches.

The first monasteries were probably established in Wales shortly before 500, spreading rapidly during the next century to Ireland from where missionaries brought the faith back to northern Britain. In this period, numerous Celtic saints were adopted by the Christian Church, the earliest being St. Dyfrig (*Duvrigg*) or Dubricius whose churches are mainly situated in the area served by the Wye River, in Southeast Wales.

"The Sacred Sites of Wales" take you on a journey around Wales, from Tintern Abbey in the southeast, to the shrine of St. Winifred in Holywell, in the northeast. It covers many of the ancient burial grounds, but is mainly centered on the six cathedrals of Wales: St. Woolos, Llandaff, Brecon, St. David's, Bangor, and St. Asaph.

Tour Nr. 1. Tintern Abbey and the Wye Valley

Most people come into Southeast Wales via the Severn Bridges, arriving first at Chepstow (*Cas-Gwent::Kass Gwent*) This is a border region in which the Romans and later the Normans made their presence felt most strongly. The gentle scenery of the Wye Valley and the fertile lands that stretch down to the Severn Estuary shelter a Roman amphitheatre, baths and barracks, ruined abbeys, impressive medieval fortifications, and delightful manor houses in which one can relive the days of the period of the Civil Wars. It is here, in the ancient county of Gwent (Monmouthshire) that we begin our pilgrimage.

    As you enter Wales, look for the signs "Croeso i Gymru" *(Croyso Ee Gumree):* Welcome to Wales."as you cross the River Severn, and have fun reading the bi-lingual traffic signs. Lovers of Henry Vaughan, the 17th Century poet, may notice that the Welsh word for automobile is curiously rendered by the Ministry of Transport as *Cerbyd : Kerrbid:*, the title of one of Vaughan's Welsh poems in which he uses the term to describe a chariot. We soon leave the motorway, however, for It is time to make our first detour: the scenic Wye Valley and Tintern.

Traveling the A466 north, we soon arrive at some of the most photographed ruins in Britain, those of Tintern Abbey, nestled snugly on the banks of the Wye below those wooded hills made famous by poet William Wordsworth. Originally built by the Cistercians in 1131, Tintern is the most complete of the ruined abbeys of Wales. Much of it was rebuilt in the 13th to 15th century at which latter time it was the largest and wealthiest monastic foundation in the principality.

After 400 prosperous years at Tintern, the Cistercians left the Abbey at its dissolution in 1536 at which time all articles of value were catalogued, weighed, and sent to King Henry VIII's treasury. The ruins then decayed in magnificent obscurity until 1782, when the publication of the Reverend William Gilpin's *Observations on the River Wye* began the trickle of visitors to Tintern that became a flood after the paintings of William Turner and the writings of William

Wordsworth had made the ruined Abbey known throughout Britain.

Today's visitors come to admire the great decorated church and the exquisite tracery of its windows. Little known is that William Herbert, the first Welshman to have addressed the House of Commons, wanted to establish a college in the Abbey in the 1590's shortly after the Dissolution. The area was also the site of a wire works that lasted from its founding in 1566 right up to 1900, thus making it sacred, in a special way, to those who study industrial history.

After enjoying the awe-inspiring remains of the Abbey; the woodland scenery in the hills around Tintern; and after paying our respects those who built the magnificent edifice (and lamenting the depradations of the Dissolution and the Reformation), we retrace our journey to pick up the Motorway M4 at Chepstow.

On our way, for perhaps the finest view of the Wye valley, with its horseshoe bend, and the Severn Road Bridge in the distance, visit St. Arvans (a mile north of the racecourse on the A466 towards Monmouth) and take the short detour to the Wyndcliff, much beloved by tourists in the last century for its romantic setting. We now head west to enter the town of Newport, the site of our first cathedral.

Peter N. Williams

Tour Nr. 2: St Woolos Cathedral, Newport

The town of Newport (Casnewydd: *Kassnweitht*), a busy industrial and commercial hub, is the third largest town in Wales (c.120,000 pop). It is not a priority on most tourists' itineraries, seemingly having little to offer the visitor. But there is lots to see here, and it is here that we visit our first cathedral.

Situated on Stow Hill, overlooking the town center is the least-known of the Welsh cathedrals and probably the least visited: St. Woolos. This is the most modern of the six cathedrals of Wales, having been a Parish church until 1921. It did not receive the status of a full cathedral until 1949, following the formation of the Diocese of Monmouth. The church is named after a fifth-century Welsh nobleman, *Gwynllyw* : *Gwin Thlee-oo*, lord of Gwynllwg *Gwinn Thloog*, who converted to Christianity after the fulfilment of his dream that he would find a white ox with a black spot on a nearby hill.

The hill was Stow Hill, and Gwynllyw built the first church there. In a heavily anglicized area that was also one of the first provinces of Wales to be controlled by the Normans, the name Gwynllyw, or Wentlooge, was quickly corrupted to Woolos. Gwynlliw and his wife Gwladys had the enviable reputation of practicing cold water bathing in the Usk all year-round, preceded and followed at night by a mile long walk in the nude. Alas, there is no record of any local Peeping Tom.

In the latter part of the twelfth century, another church was erected on Stow Hill by Norman Lord Robert Fitzhamon. This lasted until mid-fifteeenth century, when fighting involving Welsh patriot Owain Glyndwr against the Norman rulers of Wales led to its almost total destruction. The north and south aisles were then rebuilt and the tall tower was added. The columns of the fine Norman arch that remains are believed to have come from the Roman fortress at nearby Caerleon.

The nave retains many of its original Norman features, while the Lady Chapel shows evidence of being built on the site of the first church; its walls show pre-Norman influences. On the West exterior of the cathedral, you should look for a headless statue that may represent Jasper Tudor, said to have built part of the tower but more famous for being the uncle and guardian of the future king, Henry VII.

Before leaving Newport, we should have a look at a place most sacred to those interested in industrial history and the story of the Chartists, for it was here in 1839 that British troops, hastily shipped in from Bristol, and armed and waiting in the Westgate Hotel, bloodily supressed the great uprising led by John Frost and others in the tumultuous days before Parliamentary reform The sad day's terrible events are now commemorated by a series of sculptures in Westgate Square.

Our next place of pilgrimage is the much older, and perhaps more impressive Cathedral at Llandaff, near Cardiff not much more than a half-hour journey westwards out of Newport.

Tour Nr. 3: Llandaff (*Thlan daff*) Cathedral

Most visitors to Wales eventually find themselves in Cardiff (*Caerdydd : Kire deethe*) the nation's attractive and fast-growing capital city. In addition to its magnificent Civic Center, imposing Norman castle, and the re-developed dock areas at Cardiff Bay, they will find the National Museum of Wales as well as the Welsh Folk Museum. They will also find, just two miles northwest of the city centre complex, the much restored cathedral of Llandaff, situated in the village of the same name.

Unlike most Welsh churches, Llandaff is named not after a saint, but after the area in which it is located. The name translates as "Church on the River Taff." Situated on one of the oldest Christian sites in the British Isles, the cathedral was begun in the 12th Century but rebuilt and modified over and over again throughout its history. During a bleak, terrible night in January 1941, a huge German mine exploded, destroying much of the cathedral, and it was not until the 1960's that restoration was completed. Llandaff Cathedral once again took it all in stride; its whole history is one of destruction and reconstruction, of tragedy and triumph.

The cathedral is built in a hollow on a site that was probably the scene of ancient Celtic worship, for Romano-British burials have been found there. The first Christian edifice to occupy the site may have been founded in 560 by St. Teilo, bishop of South Wales who died around the year 580. Teilo built his church where a small Christian community existed founded by Dyfrig a generation earlier.

The three saints connected with the church's early foundation, Teilo (*Tielow*), Dyfrig (*Duvrigg*), and Euddogwy (*Eye thog wee)* are commemorated by the three bishops' mitres on the coat of Arms of the diocese of Llandaff. Norman Bishop Urban began building the present cathedral in the year 1120 when the Normans were consolidating their rule in that part of the country, but only very little remains of that early edifice apart from a Norman arch and traces of some windows.

The greater part of the present cathedral, including the nave and chancel arcades, the West front and the chapter house were completed by 1250. They were quickly followed by the Lady Chapel, erected during the bishopric of William de Braose. Llandaff is unique among the cathedrals of Britain as having no transepts (and for the initiated in these matters, neither does it possess a triforium). A great deal of strengthening and rebuilding then took place in the 14th century which had to last for over 300 years, during which neglect and decay saw the cathedrals's almost total destruction.

Pilgrimages to St Teilo's shrine helped support the church with their offerings until the Reformation, when they were forbidden. During the English Civil Wars, it was reported that Cromwell's soldiers, in their usual lack of regard for the sacred, used the nave as a tavern and post office and the font as a pig and horse trough. They also burned the cathedral's priceless collection of books. And, of course, any statuary, icon, or stained glass within reach of a sword, halberd or pike were ruthlessly destroyed.

More destruction was to follow. In the early part of the eighteenth century, unusually fierce storms wrecked havoc on the already crumbling building, causing the roof of the nave to fall in and the southwest tower to collapse. Restoration began under John Wood of Bath in the latter part of the century and again in 1835 under John Prichard when a curious Italian temple built by Wood inside the walls was removed and much decorative work added (all of which was destroyed by the Luftwaffe in 1941).

In the 1960's the striking parabolic concrete arch that so dominates the interior of the cathedral was completed by George Pace, surmounted by a cylindrical organ case bearing a huge Christ in Majesty (*The Majestas*) worked in unpolished aluminum.by world-renowned sculptor Jacob Epstein. Behind the high altar, the great Norman arch built by Bishop Urban in 1120 is also dominant. The tomb of St.Teilo was restored in the 19th century.

Of interest are also the Illtyd (*Ithtid*) Chapel, dedicated to the memory of the 53rd Welsh Infantry Division; the Rossetti Triptych; the font; a painting by Murillo *Madonna and Child;* the Teilo Chapel; the Lady Chapel; and the lovely stained glass windows from some of Britain's most distinguished post-war craftsmen and artists. A relic of the pre-Norman church is also on display, the tenth-century Celtic Cross that was hidden from Cromwell's soldiers but rediscovered in 1870 as part of a wall and now situated in the south aisle. In 1992 a new peal of thirteen bells was placed in the north-west tower with each bell named after a Celtic saint.

The survival of Llandaff is a miracle indeed. Visitors of today can only marvel at what has remained and been restored. Twelfth century visitors included such notaries as Geoffrey of Monmouth, who died here in 1154, and Archbishop Baldwin, who came here in 1188 to preach the Third Crusade accompanied by Giraldus Cambrensis (*Gerald of Wales*). Legend has it that one saint buried here, Dyfrig (*Duvrigg* or Dubricius is the bishop who crowned Arthur as King of Britain.

When Dyfrig's bones, brought here by Bishop Urban after being exhumed from Bardsey Island (*Ynys Enlli : Uniss Enthllee*) in the far north, were washed by the monks, the water bubbled as if a red-hot stone had been thrown into it. St. Teilo, the cathedral's founder, is also buried here; to swear upon his tomb was considered to be an extremely solemn oath upon which, over the centuries, many a contract was sealed. In 1736 one of the architects helping restore the cathedral opened St. Teilo's coffin and saw the corpse wrapped in leather, still sound, with his pastoral staff, pewter cross and chalice safely in place by his side.

Llandaff is indeed a sacred spot and a veritable treasure trove of Welsh history. We now continue our journey.

Tour Nr. 4: Tinkinswood, St. Lythan's

The sacred places of Wales are found everywhere in the principality; some of them date back a very, very long time. The huge stone monuments dotted around the landscape—the neolithic chambered tombs—are known in Welsh as *cromlechi*. Some of these are almost 5,000 years old, as old as the first pyramids of Egypt. As burial places, they were sacred to the people who built them, for it is believed that they were also centers of religion and its accompanying rituals. Two of the most well-known uncovered tombs are found near Cardiff: *Tinkinswood* and *St.Lythan's*, both only a short distance from St.Fagan's

Tinkinswood Long Cairn, established as a "Cotwold-Severn type,": is an impressive and quite well-preserved burial chamber dating back around 6,000 years or more. In it were found the bones of some 50 people as well as pottery and flint tools. Most astonishing is the size of the capstone, about 8 yards by 3 yards, estimated to weigh about 50 tons, and thought to be the largest in Britain. The chamber is approached through a walled forecourt and slab-lined entrance.

To get to Tinkinswood, which is not clearly signposted, leave Cardiff by the Cowbridge Road (A 48) and turn off at the village of St. Nicholas. After visiting the chamber, turn towards Dyffryn (*Duffrin*) Gardens (A 4226) and make a left turn on a side road that leads back to St. Nicholas. Here you will find (again not clearly marked) the second remarkable long cairn in the area: St. Lythan's Burial Chamber.

A megalithic long barrow, St. Lythan's has been long stripped of its earth covering, but the three upright stones and huge capstone remain. It is reputed to have been erected around 6200 B.C. Certain magic properties have long been associated with St. Lythan's: on Midsummer Eve, the capstone is said to rotate three times; at Hallowe'en the stones are reputed to make wishes come true. The field in which the cromlech stands is known as the "Accursed Field," reputed to be less fertile than most others in the area.

Our next visit is to Llantwit Major (Llanilltyd Fawr: *Thlanithtid Fawr)*, situated a few miles west of Cardiff International Airport, just beyond St. Athan.

Peter N. Williams

Tour Nr. 5: Llantwit Major

Llantwit Major is an anglicization of the older Celtic that was named after St. Illtyd (*San Ith tid*) a teacher and craftsman who arrived here from Brittany to preach the gospel in the 6th century. It was here that Illtyd, "the most learned of the Britons in knowledge of the scriptures" founded both a monastery and a school of divinity. The scholars included Gildas, the 6th century historian; St. Paul Aurelian; the bard Taliesin; St. Patrick (formerly Maewyn); and perhaps St. David, the patron saint of Wales. It was also here that St Samson of Dol was educated, whose *Life* is the earliest of a Welsh saint and who became the most illustrious saint of the Church in Britanny.

The Dissolution took care of what was left of fhe monastery, the school not having survived beyond the Norman invasions, but the remaining double-nave church is full of interest. One early Norman part was the parish church; the other late 13th century building served as the monastery church. A collection of Celtic stones and wheeled crosses is found in the earlier part; one of these is known as the Cross of St. Illtyd. Also of interest are the ancient curfew bell, effigies of medieval priests and an Elizabethan lady and child. In the later church are some fine murals with religious themes.

The best way to reach Llantwit is to take the A48 west from Cardiff and then south on A4222 to Cowbridge and the B4270 to the coast.

Continuing our pilgrimage to the Sacred Places of Wales, we now travel westwards, to Swansea, Wales's second largest city, to visit the Gower Peninsular.

Tour Nr. 6: The Gower Peninsular:

From our base in Swansea, it is only a short distance to Oystermouth, where we begin our tour of the Gower. Only fifteeen miles long by four to eight miles broad, officially designated in 1956 as the first Area of Outstanding Natural Beauty in Britain, the peninsular contains three National Nature Reserves and 21 sites of special scientific interest. Much of its scenic lands are owned by the National Trust and are thus preserved from unsightly development. Once the home of many animals now extinct, Gower was also home to primitive man: Palaeolithic remains have been found in caves such as Paviland.

On our circular tour, we travel west through Bishopston, noting the very English character of the place names in this part of south Gower, for this was Norman territory, not

Welsh. Near Pennard is the village of Parkmill with its Parc le Breose Burial Chamber. At Reynoldstone, on a high ridge of open common land known as Cefn Bryn (*Kev'n Brinne*) can be seen Maen Ceti, *Mine Ketti* known in English as Arthur's Stone — a large burial chamber capstone formed of a block of millstone grit, 14 ft by 7 ft, weighing about 25 tons. Legend has it that the capstone was thrown to its present location from a spot seven miles away by king Arthur, who was troubled by the "pebble" in his shoe.

For centuries, girls wishing to test the faithfulness of their lovers have been known to crawl at night round the stone at least three times, on their hands and knees, willing their lovers to appear. If the young men failed to show up, then this was a sure sign of their ineligibility as future husbands. The ghost of King Arthur is said to appear from time to time around the massive cromlech. Just down the road (A 4118) towards Penmaen (*Pen Mine*) is another large burial chamber, consisting of a deep forecourt, a gallery with two pairs of side cells, and an oval cairn.

The next stop on our pilgrimage beckons — St. David's in Pembrokeshire, in the far west of Wales. On our way, however, we must stop for a short while at Laugharne, the place most often connected with Swansea-born poet Dylan Thomas, thus a spot most sacred to all who love modern literature.

Peter N. Williams

Tour Nr. 7: Laugharne, Carmarthenshire

The fame of Laugharne (*Talacharn: Tal a ckarn*) has been spread throughout the world by its association with Dylan Thomas, who died in 1953 in New York City. To get to this charming, little town with its imposing castle ruins and its "heron-priested shore," we need to bypass the towns of Swansea and Carmarthen and then turn towards the coast at St. Clear's.

Laugharne (pronounced *Larne* in English) has become a busy little town that takes full advantage of the thousands of tourists who come to see where Dylan wrote much of his poetry and where Brown's Hotel on the main street was the site of many a drunken binge involving Dylan (pronounced *Dulan)* and his wife Caitlin (an Irish name pronouned *Kathleen).*

Dylan's unpretentious grave in the little churchyard; the beautiful walk along the tidal estuary of the River Taf, where the little fishing boats still "tilt and ride"; past the castle and up the steep hill to the the boathouse, where he and Caitlin lived and loved and fought together, with its accompanying paper-strewn and empty-beer- bottle-littered shack where the enigmatic, gifted. untidy wretch of a man wrote many of his minor masterpieces.

An annual July festival now takes place in Laugharne to celebrate Dylan's work, but the town was also home for a time to lesser-known but important Welsh writer Edward Thomas.(1878-1917) whose *Beautiful Wales* contains a number of Carmarthenshire folk songs and poems. Summertime tourist traffic brings chaos to the narrow streets of Laugharne, but we can find escape in the lonely fields and lanes on our way westward to our next sacred spot in coastal south Pembrokeshire.

Tour Nr. 8: Caldey Island and St.Govan's Chapel.

From the picturesque resort town of Tenby, in southern Pembrokeshire, with its medieval and Tudor buildings and town walls, boats will take you to Caldey Island where monks at the modern Cistercian Monastery, built alongside the 12th century priory, create their home-made perfumes and chocolate and provide a hearty welcome for visitors.

After returning to the mainland, you can visit one of the finest and best preserved medieval strongholds in Wales at Manorbier (southwest of Tenby off the A4139), famous as the birthplace of Geraldus Cambrensis, the 12th century historian and patriot; but also the spot where, according to her biographer, Virginia Wolfe first decided to take up writing.

St. Govan's Chapel:

Not too far from Tenby, out on the spectacular southwest coast of Wales, wedged into a tiny crevice in a steep cliff is another sacred spot. This is the tiny chapel of St. Govan, built in the 13th century on the site of the cell of a 6th century Celtic monk. Here the hermit St. Govan, from Wexford in Ireland, and abbot there, reportedly hid from his pagan persecutors in a niche in the rock which miraculously opened and closed behind him. The modern visitor slim enough to turn around in the niche is assured of good luck and the fulfilment of his wishes. A former well on the chapel floor was supposed to cure many diseases. A huge boulder outside the chapel is also said to hide a silver bell, stolen by pirates (or Vikings) from the chapel tower, but recovered by angels and now kept safe in the rock.

On the way down to the tiny chapel, a steep flight of stone steps cut into the steep cliff has to be navigated; legend has it that the number counted going down never matches the number reached on the way up. The whole experience is one of mystery; the site being almost inaccessible from land and sea (especially now that the Government uses much of the land approaches to the shrine as a firing range for the military). We have but one small side-journey to make on the way to St. David's, to Nevern.

Tour Nr. 9: St. Brynach's Church, Nevern

On the journey to St.David's (*Ty Ddewi : Tee Thewee,* at the edge of the most westerly peninsular of Wales, through largely unspoiled and peaceful countryside, the traveller may discern, on the flanks of the Preseli hills a large quarry from where the famous inner circle of blue stones at Stonehenge were taken so many centuries ago.

A short detour will bring us to St Brynach's Church at Nevern, (*Nanhyfer)*, a little village tucked away in the valley of the river Nyfer. Brynach is also known as *Brynach Wyddel : Brunn ack Withel)* "the Irishman," though he was a native of Pembrokeshire and spent many years in Britanny following a pilgrimage to Rome. On his feast day, 7 April, it is said that the first cuckoo arriving in Wales sings its very first song from the top of 13-ft high elaborately-patterned Great Celtic cross, dating from the tenth century, and perhaps the finest in Wales.

The church itself is on the site of one of the earliest Christian places of worship in the country, founded in the 5th century by St. Brynach after he is said to have spoken with angels on the summit of nearby Mynydd Carningli (*Muneethe Carn Inglee*:,"The Mount of Angels." It became an important stopping place for pilgrims on the way from Holywell in the northeast, to St. David's in the southwest.

It is from this time that the Celtic word Llan *Thlan* appears, signifying a church settlement and usually followed by the name of a saint, as in Llandewi *Thlan Dewee*; or

Llangurig *Thlan Girrig* , named after St David and St. Curig; but sometimes by the name of a disciple of Christ, such as Llanbedr (Thlan Bedder), named after St. Peter, or even St. Mary (*Llanfair* :*Thlan Vire*.

The churchyard contains a magnificent line of ancient "bleeding yews" and cypress trees. One of the church's famous collection of Celtic memorial stones, to Maelgwyn (*Mile Gwinn*), and now found inside the building, is inscribed in both Latin and Ogham script. Near the church, In a little leafy, narrow lane, cut into a rock, is a wayside pilgrim's cross where travelers stopped to pray for a safe journey.

It is now time to visit the site considered to be the most sacred spot in Wales, the burial place of its beloved patron saint.

Tour Nr. 10: St.David's (*Ty Dewi: Tee Dewee*), and St. Non's Well.

In the medieval kingdom of Dyfed, we find the largest church in Wales and the shrine of St.David situated in the smallest city in the British Isles. Wales did not adopt St. David as its patron saint until the 18th Century, with the reputed date of his death March lst chosen as the day of a national festival, but very little is known about him for certain except that he lived in the 6th Century and probably died in 589. Information concerning his life comes from the Latin *The Life of St. David* written in the late llth Century by Rhygyfarch but supplemented by Geraldus Cambrensis around 1200.

There are many legends concerning Dewi, as the saint is known in Welsh. In his *Life,* it is claimed that he was the son of mother Non and father Sandde, whose father, in turn, was the King of Ceredigion. Non later became a nun in Britanny where she is buried. Tradition has David's birth at St.Non's Bay (where some believe that St.Patrick was also born). Because of his frugal diet of bread and water, Dewi was known as *Aquaticus* (Water man). One story is that, while he was preaching at the Synod of Llanddewibrefi *(Thlan Dewee Brevee)*, the ground rose up beneath him so that all present could see and hear him.

The humble cleric's fame as a missionary reached Ireland and Brittany, and from the early 12th Century the church named for him at Ty Dewi *(Tee Dewee*: became a place of pilgrimage. In 1120 he was officially recognized as a Catholic saint by Pope Calixtus who declared that two pilgrimages to St. David's equalled in merit one visit to Rome. Three visits to St.David's equalled one to Jerusalem itself. In 1398 Archbishop Arundel ordained that March 1st, Dewi's feast day, be kept by every church in the Province of Canterbury. Signified by the wearing of a leek (some deign to wear a daffodil), it is solemnly celebrated by Welsh people all over the world.

For many centuries, the tiny settlement of St. David's remained one of the most important and most visited sacred places in the whole of the British Isles. Even the Norman overlord of the whole of Britain, William the Conqueror, came here to worship. The shrine of St. David also attracted Geraldus Cambrensis, who sought the bishopric and who made three unsuccessful appeals to Rome to get it, his appeals being denied by a Pope not anxious to see a Welsh Church independent of Canterbury.

Other noteworthy visitors were Bishop Houghton, Lord Chancellor to King Edward III who earned his fame by being excommunicated by the Pope whom he in turn excommunicated from the cathedral steps; Henry II, who prayed there for victory on his way to Ireland and who returned to give thanks for his successes; Bishop Ferrar, who was burned at the stake during the reign of Mary; and Bishop Davies, who procured the first Welsh translation of the Bible.

Like its counterpart at Llandaff, St.David's has also suffered the ravages of time and human folly. The cathedral building itself, the largest and most impressive among its Welsh counterparts, sits in a hollow, Glyn Rhosyn (*Glinn Hrossin)* through which runs the river Alun.(*Alin)*. It is believed by many that the placing of the cathedral was to hide it from Viking raids as it cannot be seen from the sea, but the founding of the religious settlement dates back much farther than the time of the Norsemen. In 55 A.D., David is said to have transferred his monastery from Whitesand Bay to the little valley of the Alun.

In 1088, despite the secluded, half-hidden situation, the little settlement suffered the indignity of being sacked by Vikings, raiding up and down the Welsh coast at will; at various time in later years she also suffered grievous damage from earthquakes. No traces remain from the early founding, however, much of the present church dating back only to 1180.

Less than forty years later the central tower collapsed, destroying the transepts and choir, but these were soon rebuilt. Bishop Gower (1328-1342), the remains of whose magnificent palace can be visited on the Cathedral grounds, added much to the church, including decorated windows and part of the restored central tower. He is also responsible for the magnificent Rood Screen and is buried inside the church.

During the English Civil War, Cromwell's troops were busy in their usual iconoclastic manner destroying much of the cathedral and its contents, and it was necesary for rebuilding programs undertaken by John Nash in the late eighteenth century, and by Sir Gilbert Scott in the nineteenth.

Neither architect was able to do much about the slope in the floor which rises 14 feet from the West door up to the high altar (local legend says the slope was deliberately planned to get the congregation nearer to heaven). The entrance to the cathedral is through an impressive, ruined gateway and down a steep flight of stone steps known locally as "the 39 Articles."

There is much to see and ponder over at St David's, and thus a guide book is essential. The cathedral contains the shrines of St.Caradog and St.Justinian as well as St.David (though the latter may not actually be buried there according to recent scientific tests of the bones). It also houses one of the only surviving medieval Bishop's thrones in Britain. Edmund Tudor, father of Henry VII is also commemorated here by an impressive altar-tomb.

In addition to the remains of Bishop Gower's opulent residence, the cathedral grounds also contain the ruins of St. Mary's College, for secular priests, which John of Gaunt helped found in 1377. Bishop Gower built his palace in 1340; two hundred years later, another bishop had the lead from the roof slowly stripped away to provide dowries for his five daughters —all of whom married later bishops!

Non's Well and Chapel:

Before leaving the area of the cathedral, we should visit the ruined chapel and holy well of St.Non, reputed to be

David's mother. To get there, we must travel about a mile up a narrow lane to the very edge of the steep cliffs skirted by the pathway that is part of the Pembrokeshire Coast National Park. Here, just down the hill from an ugly grey building that serves as a religious retreat, in a field usually full of cattle or horses, are the scanty remains of the ancient chapel. Nearby, almost hidden in the undergrowth is St.Non's Well. Not visited by many these days, and often full of muddy, brackish water, the well was an important place of pilgrimage for many centuries; its supposed healing powers were second only to those at St.Winifred's at Holywell in North Wales.

Peter N. Williams

Tour Nr. 11: Pentre Ifan *(Pentray Eevan)*, and Costell Henllys

The little sea-side resort of Newport, an ancient town on the estuary of the River Nevern, can be reached on the A487 north from Fishguard (Abergwaun: *Aber Gwine*) or south from Cardigan (Aberteifi: *Aber Tie-vey*). Overlooking the town on the slopes of Carn Ingli are the remains of an iron-age fort and pre-Christian hut circles. Going north, less than two miles out of Newport, where a side road leads to Nevern, you will see the sign pointing to Pentre Ifan on the opposite side of the road. A small lane, unsuitable for buses or coaches, leads up to a small lay-bye where you can park for a brief walk across the fields to the burial chamber, situated in isolated splendor on a ridge overlooking the mysterious Preseli Mountains.

The word *Pentre* in Welsh signifies village: translated literally it means "head" or" end of the town." Who Ifan was is unknown, but the impressive structure (said to be the finest in Britain) dates back to a time earlier than 2.000 BC. The earth mound has all been eroded away to expose a massive capstone (over 16ft in length) supported by huge, though spindly-seeming uprights, some of them worn to a point at the top, leaving the impresssion that the capstone is precariously balanced (though in Victorian times it was the custom for well-dressed ladies and gentlemen to enjoy picnics seated on the flat top).

In the vicinity of Pentre Ifan is another historic site worth our attention: just off the A487 to Cardigan, and visible from the road, is Castell Henllys (*Casteth Hen thleese*), an Iron-Age and Romano-British Hill fort partly excavated and partly reconstructed to show the kind of huts lived in, the various crafts and animal husbandry practiced and so on. On the A487 heading east just after you leave Newport (which is twinned with Annapolis, Maryland) is the Golden Lion (Llew Aur: *Thlew Ire*) an attractive pub with full catering and overnight facilities.

Reluctantly, we now leave Southwest Wales, the land of mystery and magic *(Gwlad hud a ledrich : Goolad heed a led rick)*, and the Pembrokeshire Coast National Park.to take the road to Newport, and the sacred site of Pentre Ifan. We now head eastwards across Wales in the direction of Brecon. On our way, we detour to a very sacred spot: for on the banks of the Teifi *(Tie-vee)*, a few miles outside Tregaron *(Tray Garron,* in Cardiganshire, we find the ruins of the abbey at Strata Florida.

Tour Nr. 12: Strata Florida (Ystrad Fflur)

The unusual name Strata Florida is a Latinised form of the Welsh Ystrad Fflur (*Uh strad fleer: Wide valley or plain of flowers*. The Abbey was founded by the Cistercian Order in 1164 though there is evidence of an earlier Cluniac settlement nearby. Local Welsh chieftain Rhys ap Gruffydd is responsible for the existing church, though parts of the present-day ruins date from later centuries. In addition to its prestige as the religious and educational centre of all Wales in the 12th and 13th Centuries, the Abbey, considered wholly Welsh in character, was also the country's political center for a short time.

The year 1238 saw an assembly of Welsh princes at Strata Florida to swear allegiance to Prince Llewelyn's son Dafydd (Dafydd ap Gruffudd). The meeting marked one of the high points of Welsh resistance to English domination before the tragic events of the Edwardian conquest. Despite this claim to fame, however, after experiencing great wealth and influence during the later centuries (mainly due to its extensive flocks of sheep and its skilful management of the wool trade), the abbey was abandoned during the rebellion of Owain Glydwr; the Dissolution that followed shortly after left only a grass-swept ruin.

Among the clutter of 18th century farm buildings that now cover most of the Abbey's original site stands a fine celtic-Romanesque west door that has a series of remarkable embellishments including triskel motifs. What makes the site so sacred, however, are not the scant remains of the Abbey, but the fact that much of the *Brut y Tywysogion* (*Britt uh Two iss Ogion: Chronicle of the Princes*) was written here. Of equal importance, the Abbey's grounds contain the reputed burial site of the greatest of all Welsh love poets, Dafydd ap Gwilym (*Dahvith ap Gwilum*).

At the time of Chaucer in England and just following that of Dante in Italy, Wales had its own "world-class" master of the poetic art. Many modern writers see Dafydd (1320-70) as

the greatest Welsh poet of all time, but certainly the most distinguished of medieval Welsh poets. Dafydd created poetry that fully equalled that produced in either England or the continent. As exemplified by his works, the period was one of the most glorious times in Welsh literary history. It is thus fitting that Strata Florida occupy a place of honor among our sacred places of Wales.

To reach Strata Florida, drive south out of Aberystwyth on the A487 and branch off at Southgate on the B4340. following the winding, mountain road through Trawscoed (*Trows coid*) to Pontrhydfendigaid (*Pont h'reed Vendig ide*) where you will see the signs pointing to the ruined abbey. It can also be reached via the B4343 from Tregaron. We now continue on our way to Brecon through some of the most delightful scenery in the British Isles — the wild, mostly uninhabited countryside around Mynydd Epynt (*Munith Epp int*) and reaching the borders of Brecon Beacons National Park.

Tour Nr. 13: Brecon Beacons National Park

The Brecon Beacons are full of interesting neolithic remains, not the least are the many standing stone circles of which Nant Tarw (*Nant Taroo*) provides a good example. In the circles, fifteen stones survive of the original twenty: they are found alongside the stream of the same name, one of the headwaters of the River Usk Outside the western circle there is a massive outlying stone, and two small uprights. The whole groups is located three miles south of Mynydd Bach Trecastell (*Munith bach traycasteth*) on the A40 between Llandovery (*Thlan Doveree)* and Trecastle (*Tray Castle*).

Cerrig Duon (*Kerrig Dee-on*) is a rather rare oval circle of 22 low standing stones in a fairly regular circle with about eight stones now missing (only about ten of its kind exist in Britain) You can find the circle on a hillside in the high, empty moorlands on the mountain road that joins up with the A4067 from Trecastle to Craig y Nos (Krige uh Noce) in the Black Mountains. In association with the circle is the high single stone Maen Mawr (*Mine Mowr*) to the north. On the east of the road is another standing stone.

Tour Nr. 14: Brecon Cathedral.

Most visitors to Brecon come here for the annual Summer Jazz festival, one of the largest musical gatherings of its kind in the world, but we are here on a different mission. Brecon's Welsh name is *Aberhonddu* (*Aber Hon Thee : head of the River Honddu*). It is a pleasant market town of under 10,000 population.

Briefly, the town dates back to the Roman occupation of Britain; was the 5th Century headquarters of the Welsh chief Brychan; is the site of a Norman castle; was attacked by Prince Llewelyn the Last and Owain Glyndwr; became an important center of the woolen industry in the 15th century; was the birthplace of Sir David Gam of Agincourt fame (and the model for Shakespeare's Fluellen), and also gave us the founder of Jesus College, Oxford (Dr.Hugh Price); the founder of the American Methodist Episcopal Church (Dr. Thomas Coke); a pair of famous actors (Charles Kemble and his sister Sarah Siddons); and a poet (Henry Vaughan, the Silurist). Opera lovers may also note that Dame Adelina Patti married her third husband here in 1898.

As Welsh cathedrals go, the one at Brecon is not ancient, dating back only to its founding as the Benedictine Priory of St.John the Evangelist at the close of the 11th Century. Giraldus Cambrensis was Archdeacon here in 1172, though not much remains of the church in which he officiated. Much of the present building dates from the 13th and 14th centuries, with Sir Gilbert Scott responsible for the extensive nineteenth-century restoration.

Like St. Woolos Cathedral at Newport, St. John's church was granted cathedral status very late in its life. The honor was granted in 1923 with the creation of the diocese of Swansea and Brecon as part of the new Church in Wales after its separation from the Church in England. Further restoration then took place, including the rebuilding of the chapel of St. Lawrence after more than 300 years of neglect and the restoration of the Harvard Chapel.

Inside the cathedral, small by English and European standards but interesting nevertheless, are found various items deserving of notice. Before the damage caused by the Reformation, the nave was divided into two by a rood screen : one half being for the use of the Benedectine monks and the other part for use as a parish church. Above the screen was suspended the Crog Aberhonndu (*Krogg Ab err Honthee: Brecon Cross)*, much celebrated in 15th century Welsh poetry for its miraculous healing powers.

Destroyed at the Reformation, the Cross, or *Golden Rood*. made the cathedral an important place of pilgrimage throughout the late Middle Ages. The Norman font, the largest in Britain is also unique for its stone cresset with 30 cups. Many of the burial slabs are decorated with medieval floreated crosses, a feature common to the region.

In 1537 the Priory of Brecon was dissolved, but fortunately the main edifice survived as the Parish Church of Brecon, remaining so until its elevation to cathedral status. Often visited for its beautiful choir vaulting, the cathedral also houses the Harvard Chapel, the regimental chapel of the South Wales Borderers (who won renown and 11 Victoria Crosses at the Battle of Rorke's Drift in the so-called Zulu War (depicted in the movie *Zulu*). The chapel also holds the Queen's Color of the 1st Battalion, thus commemorating the battle of Isandhlawana of 1879.

The cathedral also contains a rare Breeches Bible. After being silent for over 200 years, the 18th Century ring of six bells was replaced in 1995. The 16th Century tithe barn is now used as a Heritage Center and craft shop. A restaurant is also available in the cathedral grounds.

It is now time to leave Brecon Cathedral and its more than 900 years of history, and travel northwestwards to the town of Builth Wells and the tiny village of Cilmeri.

Peter N. Williams

Tour Nr. 15: Cilmeri (*Kill Merry*), Builth

For many who do more than just love Wales, Cilmeri is its most hallowed and saddest spot, for it is here, in a quiet meadow just outside the town of Builth Wells that Welsh-born native prince Llywelyn the Last (Llywelyn ap Gruffudd: *Thlew Ellin ap Griffith*) was slain. To understand the significance of Cilmeri, we must turn back in history to the Edwardian Conquest of Wales during the latter part of the 13th Century.

The ambition of King Edward was to unite the whole of the island of Britain under his kingship, and this meant he had ultimately to conquer Wales and Scotland. Prince Llywelyn had somehow managed to form a unified Wales under his leadership, but faced formidable problems in holding together all the quarrelsome parts of his kingdom. It was therefore not too difficult for Edward's much larger armies to eventually wear away the forces of Llywelyn through attrition and to impose harsh restrictions upon the Welsh leader.

At the Treaty of Aberconwy in 1277, Llywelyn was forced to accept humiliating terms and to give up most of his recently acquired lands keeping only Gwynedd west of the Conwy River. Edward followed up his successes by building English strongholds around the perimeter of what remained of Llewelyn's possessions and strong, easily defended castles were erected at Flint, Rhuddlan, Aberystwyth, and Builth garrisoned by large detachments of English immigrants and soldiers.

Prince Llewelyn was not yet finished. During a period of peace between the two leaders, his wedding to Elinor at Worcester was honored by the attendance of the English king. When the people of Wales, under his brother Dafydd, eventually rose in a massive revolt at the loss of control over their customs and their law and the restrictive and oppressive English rule, Llewelyn was the unanimous choice to lead their cause:

At first, Llywelyn's revolt was successful, the castles of Builth, Aberystwyth and Ruthin falling into his hands, and a large English force was utterly destroyed in the Menai Straights in Gwynedd. Edward was forced to devote the whole of his kingdom's resources to deal with the "malicious, accursed" Welsh, yet it was a mere chance encounter in a meadow at Cilmeri that ended the Welsh dream.

Llywelyn, separated from his army, found himself in a minor skirmish in which he was killed by an English knight unaware of the Welsh prince's identity. Upon discovery, Llywelyn's head was sent to London for display as that of a traitor. Edward's troubles with the rebellious Welsh, for all practical purposes were at an end.

Henceforth, Wales was to live under an alien political system, playing a subordinate role as an integral part of the kingdom of England. A poignant ballad by modern Welsh songwriter and nationalist Dafydd Iwan expresses the grief of the Welsh nation at the loss of their beloved Llewelyn: "*Collir Llywelyn, colli'r cyfan*" (losing Llewelyn is losing everything). Cilmeri is indeed holy ground.

In the quiet green meadow on the road from Builth Wells to Llandovery, beside the little brook, you will see a tall granite monolith. At first glance, It looks like one of the ancient standing stones erected thousands of years ago by our neolithic ancestors, yet a closer inspection reveals it to be a monument erected in 1956 to the memory of Prince Llywelyn "our last ruler" (*Ein Lliw Olaf.*

Tour Nr. 16: Machynlleth (*Mack un Thleth*)

We leave Cilmeri for our next destination Machynlleth, the delightful little town with the name that English visitors find impossible to pronounce—Machynlleth—a town that is most sacred to those who wish Wales to be independent of England so that it can govern itself and fulfil the ancient dreams of Llywelyn ap Gruffudd and Owain Glyndwr.

It was at Machynlleth in 1404 that Glyndwr, the great Welsh patriot and visionary, created his first Parliament (others were planned for Dolgellau, Harlech and Pennal). It was here that he concluded his alliance with the French king, and it was here that he revived the ancient dreams of his people, those of the Arthurian tradition first written about by Geoffrey of Monmouth that the Welsh people had nurtured in their hearts ever since.

Owain's banner was that of the *Red Dragon*, the old symbol of victory of Briton over the Saxon. In 1400, after being crowned Prince of Wales by a small group of supporters, he began his long-awaited rebellion to free his country from English dominance. By 1404, it seemed as if the long-awaited dream of independence was fast becoming a reality: three royal expeditions against Glyndwr had failed: he held Harlech and Aberystwyth, had extended his influence as far as Glamorgan and Gwent, was receiving support from Ireland and Scotland; had formed an alliance with France: he had been recognized by the leading Welsh bishops, and had summoned a parliament at Machynlleth, where he was crowned as Prince of Wales.

Then the dream died. Owain's parliament was the very last to meet on Welsh soil; the last occasion that the Welsh people had the power of acting independently of English rule. From such a promising beginning to a national revolt came a disappointing conclusion, even more upsetting because of the speed at which Welsh hopes crumbled with the failure of this alliance and the defeat of his allies.

Prince Henry retook much of the land captured by Owain, including many strategic castles. The boroughs with their large populations of "settlers," remained English in any case, and by the end of 1409, the Welsh rebellion had dwindled down to a series of guerilla raids led by the mysterious figure of Owain, whose wife and two daughters had been captured at Harlech and taken to London as prisoners.

Owain himself went into the mountains, becoming an outlaw. He may have suffered an early death, for from that time on, nothing is known of him either by the Welsh or the English. He simply vanished from sight. According to an anonymous writer in 1415," Very many say that he [Owain Glyndwr] died; the seers say that he did not." There has been much speculation as to his fate and much guessing as to where he ended his final days and was laid to rest.

Before leaving Machynlleth, be sure to visit Celtica, an exhibition that gives the story of the Celtic peoples, with special emphasis on the Celtic inheritance of modern Wales. Celtica is housed in Plas Machynlleth, dating from 1565, former home of the Marquis of Londonderry and later, the Montgomeryshire District Council. It uses the latest audio-visual technology to bring alive the sights and sounds of Wales's Celtic past. We now turn our steps to Northwest Wales, to Bardsey, the island at the very tip of the Llyn Peninsular

Peter N. Williams

Tour Nr. 17: Aberdaron and Llyn

At the very western edge of Wales, on the tip of the Llyn Peninsular, we reach Aberdaron, overlooking the sea. Here we find the small cafe known as *Y Gegin Fawr* (*Uh Geggin Vowr* :The Large kitchen) which was for centuries a hostel for pilgrims on their way to the small island just offshore named in Welsh *Ynys Enlli* (*Uniss Enthlee*: the island of strong currents*)* and its ruined Abbey of St. Mary. The name Bardsey is thought to be of Viking origin; in addition to Ynys Enlli, it is also known as The Island of 20,000 Saints.

Today the island is a nature reserve, practically uninhabited except for large colonies of seabirds. For many centuries, however, from the 5th Century onwards, Bardsey was a most important ecclesiastical center and a major place of pilgrimage, so important that two visits to Bardsey (some say three) were the equal of one to Rome. Here the first monastery was founded by St Cadfan, a Breton in 429.A.D. In the early part of the 7th Century, when Ethelfrid of Northumbria destroyed the great monastery at Bangor-is-y-

Peter N. Williams

Coed (*Bangor Ees uh Coid*) on the English borders, the surviving monks are believed to have settled here, safe on the remote, windswept island. (which today still has limited access across the treacherous straits).

The remains of the Augustinian Abbey of St. Mary date from the 13th Century. In the churchyard are the graves of some of the 20,000 saints of legend. As the very first monastic community to be founded in the whole of Britain, and as one of the most visited of the holy places in medieval Wales, the most sacred Island of Bardsey fully deserves its place on our pilgrimage.

We now turn eastwards back through the gentle, peaceful countryside of Llyn, through the majestic mountains called *Yr Eifl* : (*Ur Eye vul:the forks)* that drop abruptly into the sea. On the slopes of the east peak of the mountain is Tre'r Ceiri (*Tray'r Kayree*), "the town of Giants," the best preserved iron-age hillfort in Wales. The five acre site was originally enclosed by walls, some of whose remains still stand at 15ft high. The village dates from about the second century B.C. but was still in use at the time of the Roman occupation of Britain.

Within the walls of Tre'r Ceiri are the remains of some fifty stone huts; outside the ramparts are the well-defined cattle enclosures. To reach the fort, you take a short, but steep walk from the roadside (there is no official parking place, but you can squeeze into a narrow spot against the hedge) on the very narrow but picturesque B4417 that leads from Llanaelhaearn (*Thlan isle High arn*) to the resort village of Nefyn (*Nevin)* Turn at Llanaelhaern off the main A499 from Caernarfon to Pwllheli (*Pooth Hellee*. You will be rewarded with one of the finest mountain views in Britain.

Just at the village of Llithfaen (*Thleeth vine*), opposite the Victoria, its only pub, a narrow road takes you first up the slopes of Yr Eifl and then down a steep, narrow incline to the abandoned quarrying community of Nant Gwrtheyrn (*Nant Goorthairn*) now re-opened, after many years of abandonment and neglect, as the National Language Centre of Wales. Here one can spend time learning the Welsh language in a restored quarrymen's cottage. Weekend courses are especially popular with businessmen and adult learners.

The centre is named after the British leader Vortigern, who supposedly sought refuge here and where he was supposedly drowned, trying to escape the fires that came down from the angry Celtic gods to destroy his palace (Vortigern is held responsible for inviting the Saxons to the shores of Britain). One of the last residents of the old village helped guard Irish rebel leader De Valera in Lincoln Gaol during the early days of World War One. HIs stories of life in the village, always told in the Welsh language, enthralled many visitors to the language center in the early 1990's.

People from all parts of Wales (and many from other countries) come here to learn the Welsh language in an ideal setting. We are on our way, however, to the other Welsh religious settlement to have been named Bangor. As usual, however, there are a few very necessary stops we have to make as part of our modern pilgrimage, the first one at Clynnog Fawr.

At Clynnog Fawr (*Klunnog Vowr*), on the road to Caernarfon, the Church is dedicated to St. Beuno (*St. Bine-o*) Wales's second most revered saint after St. David. Completely dominating the present village, the church marks an important place of rest for medieval pilgrims on their way to or from Bardsay. Founded in 616 A.D., St Beuno's Church may have originally been monastic, but had become collegiate by the year 1291, though the present building dates only to the late 1500's after the Dissolution.

The tomb of St. Beuno was destroyed by a fire in 1856 but was restored fifty years later. Local tradition tells us that the stone with a cross was given to Beuno by a Prince of Gwynedd. The church contains a curious dugout chest known as St. Beuno's Chest. Beside the roadside not too far from the church is St. Beuno's Well, a spring where the Welsh 18th C. historian and naturalist Thomas Pennant claimed to have witnessed the healing of a paralytic.

After leaving Clynnog Fawr, to continue our journey to Bangor, we soon come to the shores of the Menai Straits (*Afon Menai : Av onn Men Aye*) that separate the island of Anglesey (*Ynys Mon: Uniss Mon*) from the Welsh mainland. A short detour off the main highway will bring you face to face with one of Edward Ist's mightiest strongholds, the castle at Caernarfon, a World Heritage Site.

Tour Nr. 18: Caernarfon (*Kire Narvon*)

It is not the castle, however impressive it may be, that makes this spot sacred to the Welsh people. In the town that grew up around it, in an area still predominantly Welsh-speaking in the 1990's, there is a high school named after Sir Hugh Owen, a nineteenth-century pioneer in education in Wales. Owen's open letter to the Welsh people in 1843 urged acceptance of the schools of the British and Foreign Schools Society, and his untiring efforts to secure a university for Wales led to a commission to promote the idea in 1854, the university itself to be established through voluntary contributions.

Owen's pleas to the government for financial help were typically unheeded, and it was public subscription that brought to fruition the centuries-old dream of Owain

Glyndwr. In 1872 Aberystwyth University opened its doors, followed by the University College of North Wales in 1894 at Bangor. Like that of Aberystwyth, the much-loved Bangor college provided the foundations in so many different areas that led to the national revival of Wales, not only in the late 1890's, but which is taking a leading part in the current revival of the Welsh language.that began in the 1960's. It is therefore, that connection with Sir Hugh Owen that Caernarfon is included in the Sacred Places of Wales.

Caernarfon contains the remains of a Roman fortress, Segontium, located one half mile southeast of Castle Square at the side of the A4085 to Beddgelert. It was founded by Agricola in 78 AD, remaining occupied until 380 A.D. The site is well-served by its small museum. Close to the Roman Mithraeum is Llanbelig Church, dedicated to Peblig (*Publicus*) the son of Magnus Maximus who claimed the title of Roman Emperor (known to the Welsh as Macsen Wledig: a national hero).

In the nearby village of Waunfawr (*Wine Vowr)* there is an impressive monument to explorer John Evans, a local man who searched for the descendants of Prince Madog among the Mandan Indians in North America in the early part of the 18th century, and whose maps of the Missouri River Basin were used by Lewis and Clark on their own expedition to the West Coast.

Tour Nr. 19: The Island of Anglesey:

The isle of Anglesey (*Ynys Mon: Uniss Mone*) is a veritable treasure-trove of sacred sites that include many early Middle-Stone Age remains. About one and a half miles from the village of Llanfair PG (*Thlan vire PG*) stands the stately mansion known as Plas Newydd (*Plars Neweethe*), former seat of the Marquesses of Anglesey, but now in the care of the National Trust. Opposite the stables is a burial chamber consisting of an 11ft by 9ft capstone and a small ante-chamber.

Two miles north from Llanfair.P.G, at the hamlet of Cefn Bach (*Kev'n Bach*) and practically unique in the whole of Britain, is the well-preserved passage grave of Bryn Cell Ddu (*Brinne Kethley Thee*: the hill of the black cells). Modern restoration of the mound only partially protects the area of the prehistoric mound 160 ft in diameter which probably covered a henge type monument.

An outer 6ft long passage and a 20 ft long inner passage lead to a polygonal chamber roofed by two huge stones. The chamber was surrounded by four concentric stone circles, three inside the cairn itself and the fourth marking the base. Inside the chamber is a replica of an incised monolith now in the National Museum of Wales, Cardiff. The curious stone, with its wavy lines and spirals was found above a pit containing burnt bones. The site may have been a place of worship as well as a burial ground.

Barclodiad y Gawres (*Barklod ee-ad Uh Gow ress*) shares the distinction of Bryn Celli Ddu as having mural artwork. Translated as '"the apron of the giantess," It is located on the western side of the Island of Anglesey on the road (A4080) between Aberffraw (Aber Frow) and the village of Llanfaelog (*Thlan Vye-log*). This is a cruciform passage grave, painstakingly excavated and restored: its five carved stones are among the finest of their kind ever found in Britain with their lozenges, chevrons, spirals and zig-zag patterns. The art style is similar to that found in the area of the Boyne, Ireland.

A 20 ft long passage leads to the central chamber, which is accompanied by side chambers. Only a part of the original 90ft diameter mound remains.

For many Welsh people, a most sacred place is the ruined 16th Century church found on the southwest tip of the island, across from the little town of Newborough. Here, on a little promontory jutting out from a vast expanse of sands and forest that makes up a nature reserve called Ynys Llanddwyn (*Uniss Thlan thooin)* is the spot where Dwynwen, patron saint of Welsh lovers, chose to make her retreat.

St. Dwynwen's Day is celebrated on January 25th. For the Welsh-speaking, it replaces St. Valentine's Day as the day to send flowers and greetings to loved ones (a point not unnoticed by today's publishers of Welsh greeting cards). A lovely legend is the story of Dwynwen's rejection of the sexual advances of her swain Maelon.

Though in love with Maelon (*My Lon*), Dwynwen's wish to remain chaste led her to dream that God offered her a sweet drink that would turn her suitor to ice and free her from her bonds to him. She was then granted three wishes. one to revive Maelon; two, to become the patron saint of lovers; and three, never to marry. What happened to the poor love-struck Maelon we will never know, but a miraculous spring, Ffynnon Dwynwen,.appeared at the spot where Dwynwen had her dream. In the spring, located in what is now a very dificult-to-locate spot on the muddy, tidal beach, fishes were said to reveal the fate of the love sick.

On the northwest side of Anglesey, on the rocky summit of Holyhead Mountain, the ancient 17-acre hill fort of Caer y Twr (*Kire Uh Toor*), uses the precipices as its defences. These are reinforced where necessary by massive dry -stone walls reaching from crag to crag on the north and east, and in some places still reaching a height of ten feet.

Below the fort is a group of about twenty enclosed huts dating from the 3nd to the 4th Century named Ty Mawr (*Tee Mour*). Some of these still contain hearths and shelves or slabs marking the position of beds. From debris found there, one of them seems to have been occupied by a copper worker. The site is reached on a minor road B4545 that circles Holy Island, on the north west tip of Anglesey, near the port of Holyhead.

Lligwy (*Thlig wee*) is an impressive neolithic burial chamber found on the eastern side of the island near the road from Menai Bridge to Amlwch (*Amlook*) and thence to Moelfre *Moyle Vray* on a side road. Lligwy's huge capstone, one of the largest in Britain, weighs about 25 tons and is supported by low uprights placed above a rock-hewn pit, making the greater part of the chamber below ground.

A large number of human remains were found at the site, as well as at the iron-age village of Din Llugwy (*Deen Thligwee*) a short distance away on the other side of the main road. The village was probably built during the closing years of the Roman occupation;it consists of circular and rectangular stone buildings inside a defensive wall.

It is now time to retrace our journey back to the mainland and to the city of Bangor.

Tour Nr. 20: Bangor

Bangor (pop. c. 12,000), is completely dominated by the university buildings high on a ridge overlooking the town. Down in the city center, however, shyly hiding from view is Bangor Cathedral, occupying the site of one of the earliest monastic settlements in all of Britain. The word *Bangor* comes from the Welsh for a wattle fence, for it was such a fence that surrounded the monastic community founded here by St.Deiniol in the year 525. Deiniol was consecrated Bishop in 546 and his church became a cathedral.

The cathedral itself merits highly on our list of sacred places, for it may be the oldest in Britain in continuous use as such. Four bishops of Bangor became Archbishops of

Canterbury. Archbishop Baldwin preached the Crusade here in 1188

The present unpretentious building, or what is left of it after centuries of neglect and numerous fires, was erected by Bishop David between 1120 and 1139. Much damage was sustained during the Welsh wars against Edward I and again in 1402 at the hands of Welsh patriot Owen Glendower's army. It wasn't until the late 15th century that extensive rebuilding took place, lots of which was again damaged or neglected during the English Civil Wars. In the nineteenth century, the ubiquitous Sir Gilbert Scott was called upon to supervise a drastic restoration which resulted in the building we see today—a Victorian creation completely hiding any vestiges of the original edifice.

Yet some items of interest remain. The cathedral's greatest treasure is the late thirteenth century *Anian Pontifical*, a service book for Bishops, set to music. Inside the church we can find a set of dog tongues (a set is also found at Clynnog Church), used to remove noisy or unruly dogs from church services; the Mostyn Christ of 1518 said to have been hidden by the Catholic Mostyn family during the Reformation; and a twelfth-century tomb once thought to have been that of Prince Owain Gwynedd, one of the few rulers of an independent Wales. He is one of three princes of Gwynedd buried here.

Inside the ancient but venerable structure, two murals depict the sacred places of our pilgrimage — the six cathedrals of Wales and also notable men of the Welsh Church from Dubricius (*Dyfrig : Duvrigg*) to the first Archbishop of Wales, A.G. Edwards. There is also a memorial to poet Goronwy Owen, who left his native Wales to teach at William and Mary College in Virginia in the mid-eighteenth century.

A very pleasant, and most unusual feature of the exterior of the cathedral is the Bishop's Garden, containing the Biblical garden which is planted on one side with flowers and shrubs traditionally associated with the medieval church. On the other side, planted chronologically according to the order in which they are mentioned, are found examples of all trees, shrubs and plants in the Bible and able to survive the climate of this northern part of Britain.

Peter N. Williams

Tour Nr. 21: Capel Garmon and Penmaenmawr (*Kappel Garmon and Pen Mine Mowr*).

Leaving Bangor, our journey now takes us eastwards, along the shores of the Menai. The Snowdon Massif is on our right, and the isle of Anglesey to our left, accessible by Telford's suspension bridge. Before reaching the coastal highway, we detour through the mountains of Snowdonia National Park to reach the much-visited tourist center of Betws y Coed and the prehistoric site of Capel Garmon.

At the National Museum of Wales in Cardiff, you can view a lst Century B.C. wrought iron firedog found at Capel Garmon, Betws-y Coed (*Bet us uh Coid*), Gwynedd. The burial chamber itself dates back to about 1500 B.C.A long barrow with three chambers, one with its immense capstone still firmly in place, the whole surrounded by surviving stone base.

Capel Garmon can be reached about one and a half miles up a small road leading northwest (at Rhydllanfair: *Rheed Thlan Vire*) from the main road (A5) from Betws Y Coed to Pentrefoelas (*Pen tray Voilas*), Capel Garmon burial chamber belongs to the Cotswold Severn Group; it is a large chamber inside a cairn, with a forecourt and blind entgrance. In addition to the iron fire dog, the tomb has yielded fragments of beakers, human bones, flnts, and a neolithic pot.

From Betws y Coed, we take the A470 north through the Vale of Conwy to reach the main coastal road at Llandudno (*Thlan did no*) Junction. We now skirt the mountains and the sea and travel by modern highway along the Welsh Riviera, a string of holiday resorts much frequented by the English summer hordes. Before we reach our next major destination, we will take a short detour west for a few miles to reach Penmaenmawr, the massive headland that dominates this part of the coast.

Druid's Circle, Penmaenmawr (*Pen Mine Mour*), Gwynedd. On the main coastal road from Bangor to Conwy(A55) you will drive in a modern tunnel through the granite headland at Penmaenmawr that for many centuries was avoided by coach travelers as being too dangerous (passengers preferred to go over the Sychnant (*Suck Nant*) Pass or wait for low tide to travel along the sands rather than face the precipitous, rocky shelf that served for a road high above the sea at Penmaenmawr). The route was dreaded by no less than the literary giant Dr. Johnston who wrote of its terrors on his visit to North Wales.

Up on the headland itself, on the slopes of just-under 2,000 ft Moelfre (*Moyle Vray*) is the so-called Druid's Circle. Nothing to do with the much later Druids, the stones are the remains of two Bronze Age circles, but for many centuries they were associated with the worship of two sinister goddesses, Andras and Ceridwen.

Nearby, on the same History Trail, is the the pre-historic axe factory at Graig Lwyd (*Grige Loo-id*). Here, flints and large arrow stones have been found; from them tools were made which found their way as far south and east as Wiltshire and Gloucestershire, and as far west as Northern Ireland.

From Penmaenmawr, on our way to the cathedral of St.Asaph, another detour off the coastal road to Chester takes us to the little church of Llanelian-yn-Rhos, situated two miles inland from the resort town of Colwyn Bay.

Tour Nr. 22: Llanelian and St. Asaph

At Llanelian yn Rhos (*Thlan Ellyan un Hrose: the Church of St. Elian*) , we find a spot that is sacred in a very special way, for it was here that pilgrims came not to be cured or to pray for those who were sick, but to curse those they considered their enemies. Even though the spring is said to have issued from the ground when the 6th Century St. Elian prayed for water to drink, the well here was known not as a holy one, but as a malignant one.

In the nineteenth Century, Ffynnon Llanelian became especially known throughout Wales as a cursing well. Visitors would write the name of their intended victim on paper through which a crooked pin was then pushed. The keeper of the well would then write the victims's name on a pebble or a lead slate which was dropped into the water.

It was a lucrative business for the custodians, for a steady supply of visitors kept the job busy right up to the early years of the present century. One well-keeper, Sarah Hughes, is said to have earned about three hundred pounds a year. She received a nice income from those who came to curse and an even nicer one from those who came to have the curses lifted.

The imprisonment of John Evans, in 1854 for "taking money by means of deception," eventually put a stop to the practice, and the well was drained and then hidden by a local clergyman in order to dissuade the members of his congregation casting spells on one another.

As a place of pilgrimage, however, especially to patriotic Welshmen, the Church of St. Elian deserves to be better known as the burial place of Ednyfed Fechan (*Ed nuv ed Veckan*, chief minister of Llewelyn the Great *(Llywelyn Fawr)*. Llewelyn's mastery at dealing with the English crown had brought a large measure of self-autonomy to his Welsh kingoms and great prestige in the courts of Europe, but his death in 1240 ended all hopes that Wales would remain independent from England. Ednyfed's descendants, nevertheless, would become great landowners in Wales and the ancestral family of the Tudors of Penmynydd.

We now leave Llanelian to swing further inland into the still very-Welsh Vale of Clwyd (Dyffryn Clwyd: *Duffrin Clue-id)*, at the head of which is the tiny town of St. Asaph (Llanelwy: *Thlan Elwy*) pleasantly situated alongside the River Elwy. On our short journey, we pass by the little village of St. George (*Llan Sain Iôr : Thaln Sign Yore)*, where the local tradition has it that this is where St.George slew the dragon.

St.Asaph's Cathedral

One surprise, upon reaching St. Asaph, is to find the cathedral situated on a hill, instead of being hidden down in a hollow as we found at St.David's, Llandaff, and Bangor. Perhaps the shrine needed to be placed in a prominent spot, for it is the smallest medieval cathedral in the British Isles. It is sacred, nevertheless, and holds a special place in the hearts of the Welsh people.

St.Asaph may have been founded as Llanelwy in the 6th Century as a monastic settlement by St.Kentigern (*San Cyndyrn : San Kund earn* in Welsh but also known as *St.Mungo*). Kentigern's successor as Bishop in 570 was Asaph, who gave his name to the city and the Diocese. In 1151 Geoffrey of Monmouth was appointed Bishop though he never visited his diocese, preferring to spend most of his time at Oxford.

In 1188, Gildas described the church as "very poor indeed," and less than one hundred years later, it was completely destroyed by the army of Edward I on his conquest of North Wales. In a major and unprecedented victory for the Welsh Church, the cathedral was then rebuilt on its original site through the efforts of Bishop Anian II despite Edward's preference for Rhuddlan : *Hrithlan* (where he established a huge fortress and where the Statute of 1284 created a dependent Wales to be governed by royal edict).

Further damage took place in 1402 during the rebellion of Owain Glyndwr, when a fire destroyed the woodwork, and again in 1715 when the tower was completely demolished in a fierce storm. Our old friend Sir Gilbert Scott was responsible for major restoration during the latter half of the nineteenth and the early part of this century. As at Bangor, it is mainly his church that you see today.

In addition to Geoffrey of Monmouth, prominent churchmen to have held the Bishopric at St. Asaph over the centuries include Bishop William Morgan, the main translator of the Bible into Welsh in the latter half of the 16th Century, which perhaps "saved" the language from degenerating into a mere peasant patois, and who is buried in the cathedral he served so well.

Others include Bishop William Lloyd, who resisted Anglicization in his diocese by ensuring the appointment of Welshmen, but remembered mostly as one of those in the reign of James II, who refused to have the Declaration of Indulgence read; and Bishop Samuel Horsley, who opposed Priestly in the Trinitarian controversy. In 1920 a momentous event occurred when then current Bishop A.G. Edwards was enthroned as the first archbishop of the newly constituted Church of Wales.

Inside the Cathedral, tiny by English standards, *(which, a most Welshmen and women know simply do not apply i North Wales in matters of architecture or language)*, there much of interest. The refurbished roof painting celebrates t investiture of Charles in 1969. though that event is fading in distant memory and becoming less glamorous and memora each passing year. The 13th Century nave of Anian II has 1 century arcades; the saint himself is remembered by an eff in the South Aisle which also contains the curious Greyho Stone with its unexplained heraldic decorations.

Here in the South Aisle is also found a tablet to memory of explorer H. M. Stanley (*of Dr. Livingstone j* whose youth as an orphan was spent at the St.A workhouse nearby, now part of the Glan Glwyd He (*Ysbyty Glan Clwyd : uss butty glan clooie*). An exqu carved ivory Madonna may have come from a galleon ill-fated Spanish Armada.

In the Chapter Treasury is a fine collection of earl and prayer books including the first Welsh New Te (1587), Bishop Morgan's magnificent Welsh Bible and many other Welsh religious books. Another interest is the Triglot Dictionary of the eccentric Robert Jones (*Dic Aberdaron)*, who traveled about the early nineteenth century with his faithful cat though unschooled, is reputed to have mastered foreign languages, ancient and modern.

It is the association with Dr. Morgan, howeve with Dic Aberdaron, that makes St.Asaph's especially sacred to all who hold the Welsh la religious traditions dear. In the cathedrals gr memorial to the small group who translated the Welsh with Bishop Morgan's name in the center.

In 1563, the London Parliament had passed a bill ordering that the Bible be translated into Welsh, an act that was not undertaken with any love or respect to the language, but one that, according to Professor Johnston, formed "an essential part of the programme of the Protestant Reformation in Britain." Elizabeth and her parliament were appalled at the slow progress in of the Welsh people in learning the English language. They thought that by having Welsh translations placed next to the English texts in Church, not only would the congregations learn Protestantism, they would also learn. English.

The reverse took place, of course, and the Welsh language was given an unintended status and a place of honor by being used as a medium for the holy scriptures. Why would a congregaton bother with English, when there was a perfectly acceptable Welsh in which to worship God? (and a book from which one could learn to read and write?). It was William Morgan, parish priest of Llanrhaeadr-ym-Mochnant (*Thlan Hrye adder um Mock Nant*, and later Bishop of Llandaff (*Thlan Dav*) and St. Asaph who gave the Welsh people what they so urgently desired.

William Morgan's birthplace, the remote Ty Mawr (*Tee Mour)* a much-secluded Welsh stone cottage, is located near Penmachno, near Llanrwst. To get there, a national Welsh shrine, one should take. the road from Bangor to Betws y Coed, and then to Penmachno (*Pen Mack No)* on the way to Llangollen: *Thlan Gothlen*).

It is but a short journey by road from the city of St. Asaph through the gap in the Clwydian *Klue Iddy un*) Hills just before they reach the Irish Sea, to a town that has no cathedral and yet is one of the most important and well-known stopping places on our pilgrimage.

Tour Nr. 23: Winifred's Well, Basingwerk and the Greenfield Valley

Holywell (Treffynnon: *Tray Funnon*) in Flintshire (less than twenty miles from Chester, on the English border) is "the town of the Holy Well." For over one thousand years, the well at Holywell was renowned throughout Britain and beyond for its healing powers, a reputation that somehow managed to survive the Reformation. During the author's boyhood, a large collection of crutches and canes left behind as a testament to the water's curative powers was a prominent feature of the site (they have since been removed by order of the Catholic Church).

The Greenfield Valley, just below Holywell is important in Welsh industrial history and its Heritage Trail is well worth a visit, as are the remains of Basingwerk Abbey, founded in 1131 as a Savignac Monastery but mostly demolished as a Cistercian House at the Reformation, with its parts scattered throughout the area to be relocated in many local churches. The vesiges that do remain give no hint of the abbey's former importance, but their situation in a large green meadow overlooking the wide Dee Estuary, is pleasant enough.

But it is to the holy well at the upper end of the Valley, just before the steep climb up the the town itself, that we make our pilgrimage. The well itself, formed from a mountain spring, is housed inside the shrine of St. Winifred (*Gwenffrwd: Gwen Frude* or *Gwenfrewi : Gwen Frewee)* regarded as the finest surviving example of a medieval holy well in Britain. The legend of St. Winifrid is responsible for the erection of the present shrine on a site chosen originally chosen by St. Beuno (*St. Bye No* for a chapel.

When a local chieftain named Caradoc (*Car Add Og*) attempted to rape Beuno's niece Gwenffrwd, she ran to the chapel for sanctuary but though she failed to reach the doors, her refusal to submit to her pursuer caused him to cut off her head in his rage. The head rolled down the hillside, a spring miraculously appearing where it came to rest in a deep hollow. Beuno reattached Gwenffrwd's head, and she lived to become an abbess (at Shrewsbury) and later, a saint. Would-be rapist Prince Caradoc, meanwhile, fell dead under the holy man's curse.

The saint was to become the patroness of virgins. The well formed from the gushing spring then became a place of pilgrimage visited by, among others, Richard lst, to pray for his Crusade; Henry V (both before and after his famous victory at Agincourt), who came on foot from Shrewsbury; and King James II, who came here to pray for a son (a prayer which was granted by the birth of the Old Pretender). It is bitterly ironic that the succcess of his prayer led to James's deposition from the throne, for the British Constitution would not allow a Catholic heir.

In the twelfth Century, the religious house at Shrewsbury (where she had spent the remainder of her days as abbess) acquired Winifred's relics, and her shrine there became a popular place of pilgrimage. In the early 15th Century, the Pope granted the right to sell special indulgences to all pilgrims visiting Holywell to the monks at Basingwerk, who took charge of the well up until the Reformation. In 1415, the feast of St. Winifred was ordered by statute to be celebrated throughout the realm along with that of St. George (of England) and St. David (of Wales).

About 1490, Margaret Beaufort, Countess of Richmond and mother of Henry VII and particularly devoted to the saint, had a new two-storied chapel built over the star-shaped well, which is covered by an ornate vault and surrounded by a processional passage. The stone walls are covered with graffitti dating back centuries that tell of miraculour cures obtained from immersion in the icy waters.

A long bathing pool fed by the spring lies in the courtyard outside the chapel, Just below the surface of the water you can see the stone of St. Beuno upon which he taught Winifred or upon which he bade farewell to her. In the valley below the well are a number of stones said to be stained with Winifred's blood or covered with a fragrant red moss miraculously renewed each year. .

St. Winifred's Well is the only shrine in Britain that has an unbroken tradition of pilgrimage since the early Medieval period. Because the well was regarded as medicinal as much as religious, the chapel escaped the merciless destruction of the Reformation itself. At the Dissolution, however, Winifred's bones bones were scattered by the agents of Henry VIII (the one finger that survived was then taken to Powys Castle and from thence to Rome, only returning to Britain in 1852).

In 1605, a group of visitors to the Well included Anne Vaux, her sister Eleanor Brooksby and others, Catholic recusants who refused to swear allegiance to James 1st as head of the Church in England. Their pilgrimage to Holywell was seen by the authorities as a cover-up for activities connected with the famous "Gunpowder Plot" to blow up the King and Parliament, an act of treason that led to untold recriminations against the country's Catholic minority and centuries of suspicion and mistrust.

On Nov 3, 1629, St. Winifred's Day, over fifteen hundred people managed to gather at the chapel, and it has continued to be an important place of pilgrimage for Roman Catholics ever since, despite many attempts to stop the practice, including the shutting down of many of the town's hotels and hostels by Chester justices in 1637. At that time, the walls of the chapel were also whitewashed and the safety railings around the well removed (more than one historian has queried — "so that pilgrims might accidentally drown?")

Only two years after King James's visit in 1686, the holy well and the chapel in which it was housed were ransacked by supporters of the ardent Protestant William III. It was later once again restored, and in 1774 was visited by the well-known literary critic Dr. Samuel Johnson on his journey around North Wales. The learned, but prudish doctor remarked on the indecency of a woman bathing there, yet the popularity of the shrine continued to attract pilgrims, over one thousand visiting during the first year of a new hospice opened in the 1880's.

Since World War II, the Well has received a new lease of life as the automobile and the motor coach (and up until the early 60's the railroad) have brought many more pilgrims (mainly Irish immigrants from Liverpool and Manchester, but some from all parts of Britain and the Continent) to partake of the healing waters and to undergo the ritual of passing three times through the inner well (this custom may date from a Celtic practice of triple immersion or it may result from a prayer written by a 12th Century prior of Shrewsbury who cautioned that more than one immersion may be necessary for a cure).

We have come to the end of our pilgrimage to the most sacred sites in Wales. From Holywell, about 16 miles west of Chester, just off the A55, it is but one hour by major highways to Manchester Airport.

About the Author

Peter N. Williams was born in Mancot, a little village in Flintshire, North Wales, just inside the border with England. Brought up in the industrial town of Flint, he was educated at King's School, Chester and at the University College, Swansea, South Wales. After arriving in the United States in 1957, he served with the US Army in Germany with an artillery unit. Following his three years of military service, he taught high school in Delaware for a number of years before completing his Ph.D. in English at the University of Delaware. He then taught English at the university before becoming chairman of the English department at Delaware Technical and Community College. He is now the editor, Welsh Desk, at *Britannia.com.*

Well known to readers of the Welsh-American newspapers Y Drych and Ninnau for his articles on Welsh history and traditions, he is a long-serving director of the National Welsh American Foundation. In 1999, he was honored for his work on behalf of Wales and Welsh Americans by being made a member of the Gorsedd at the National Eisteddfod of Wales.